KT-472-573

William Collins Sons & Co Ltd
London · Glasgow · Sydney · Auckland
Toronto · Johannesburg

**This book is for Sarah and Emma
with my love**

Also compiled by Nanette Newman

THE BEST OF LOVE
LOTS OF LOVE
VOTE FOR LOVE
ALL OUR LOVE
FACTS OF LOVE

Through the generosity of Nanette Newman,
all royalties from this book will be given to
the Invalid Children's Aid Association.

Jacket design and endpapers by Sarah Forbes

First published 1972
© Invalid Children's Aid Association
This impression 1986
ISBN 0 00 195280 3
Made and Printed in Great Britain by
William Collins Sons & Co Ltd Glasgow

GOD BLESS LOVE

A collection of children's sayings
compiled by
NANETTE NEWMAN

COLLINS

God bless my sister
And God bless Mummy And daddy
God bless my toys And friends
And Everyone in the world
And god bless love

Foreword

There is an old English proverb which says "Children pick up words as pigeons peas, and utter them again as God shall please," and I daresay every parent has at some time or another either bored or enchanted their nearest listener with the latest words of wisdom uttered by their little darlings. I am no exception to the rule and I really have no defence to offer to those readers who find the sayings of children inferior to the sayings of our elder statesmen, except that in my view children have a habit of getting to the heart of the matter without fear, favour or pomposity.

In making this selection from literally thousands of entries so generously sent in or collected from friends and schools over the country, I have tried to tread that thin line between precocity and penetrating insight. I decided to keep the contributors anonymous except for their Christian names and ages, but they are

drawn from all walks of life, from
private and State schools, different
religions and totally different
backgrounds. The only thing they share
is a common language of innocence.

I make no apology for the fact that
the title and indeed the inspiration for
the book came from my own youngest
daughter. She added a postscript to her
scrambled bedtime prayers - after the
usual list of requests she suddenly
said, "Oh, and God Bless Love."

Listening to her, it occurred to me
that most of us have travelled a long
way from something so basic and so
obvious. Perhaps children are more aware
than we are. I believe that they are
more caring and more careful and that in
many ways, while perhaps making us
laugh, they also shame us with their
honesty.

This is just a collection, nothing
more, of drawings and sayings of children
under twelve. If some of them touch you
as they touched me, then perhaps Emma's
postscript has been answered.

Nanette Newman

I think you can fall in love if you have your picture taken in frunt of the church.

Eric aged 5

love is important becaus if
people did not love each other
there wouldn't be any people.

Lynn aged 7

I know my mother and Father
love each other because my
mother cooks him his Favorite
roast every night

Theresa aged 8

you have to Love your
baby brother otherwise he
geas wind

Alice aged 4

True love is when some thing
has died and you still remember it
like my hamster.

Bobby aged 6

MY TORTUS FELL IN LOVE BUT IT MADE HIM
TIRED AND HE WENT TO BED FOR ABOUT
FOUR YEARS. I THINK LOVE DOES MAKE YOU
TIRED, SPECIALLY OLD WOMEN.
THEY ALLWAYS SLEEP A LOT.

John aged 6

Love

I think god made two many

peeple

Eric aged 7

you can only love things
near you, you can't love
countries or lots of peopl

Rose aged 6

I sometimes think I love
everything and Everybody
But I know I don't.

Soraya aged 9

If only the world were made of love.

Louise aged 7.

LOVE

sex us a part of love but not a very good part. Joanna aged 6

My mummy says my Daddy is in love with his car and when I grow up I shall have two.

Roger aged 6

I saw a book once with all drawings in it about falling in love and I think you have to have eggs.

Vera aged 5

Love is hard to do to peeple you don't perticuly like.

Deborah aged 10

Love
t makes you coff a lot

Peter aged 5

Guinea Pigs Like Peace

Emma aged 4

I would like to marry my dog.
but it isint alowed, is it?.

Bruce aged 6

Kittens

My cat falls in love and stays out
all night and then he brings a lot of
kittens back.

Henry aged 6

my aunty falls in love
when we go on holiday but
She never likes it and
She cries

Leonard aged 6

I once saw some one fall in love
In a car. It wasn't going though.

Sally aged 7

I wouldn't fall in love because girls are all spotty and they wisper

Norman aged 6

I think love mean's you have to buy stamps at the post office and when you go to the doctor he marries you free

Martha aged 6

I know what Love is, its the stuff they sell on the telly.

Clara aged 4

I dont think there should be
Rich churches when there
Are poor people

Fiona aged 11

If you eat sweets in church the vicar tells Jesus

Robert aged 5

My granny always talks to Jesus on Sundays. The rest of the week she goes to Bingo which is where he lives sometimes.

Charles aged 5.

When you go to church you put mony in the box and god loves you

Florence aged 7

I wish Jesus would come back and stop the fighting because I think they've all had enough by now.

Alan aged 7

I have been praying to god for over a year now to stop the fighting and wars but he hasn't done anything about it — yet.

Zarab aged

I feel very sad for children left alone in war an I would like to Love them but they never put their names in the paper.

Liz aged 7

Sometimes when theres lots of war they ration Love.

Tessa aged 8

I wish they Could Declare love Instead of War.

Deirdre aged 11

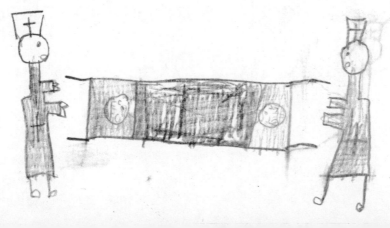

I feel sad when my Mummy
goes out and slams the Door
and leves my Daddy crying.

Tessa aged 4

mummy went away even though I loved her.

Michael aged 6

something that makes me sad

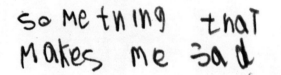

Peace

My
Peace. Mummy and daddy like

They dont often get it.

David aged 7

My brothers and sisters.

David Andrew Robin Steven Caroline Kingsley Diane

My mother said She
won't get maried again
it's too much truble

Shirley aged 5

Everybody loves baby Jesus even my uncle and both my bruthers but I don't. I love the three wizmen best becus they brout presense.

John aged 5

I had a baby when I was little. It was a brother baby but it didn't like waking up and I think they gave it away with Christmas but I am not sure. You could ask them.

George aged 8

This   is   god

If I was god I would go to all the
countries and say love each other
and stop being greedy.

Raj aged 9

I love everybody and everything
even ants. god made ants to be
loved not trodden on.

Ronald aged 7

Once I saw a Christmas tree
being put to death

Sally aged 8

You must take care
of Love — if You
Don't it goez bad

James aged 5

King Henry the eight fell in love lots
of times and in the end they
had to chop his head off because he
was geting fat.

Sidney aged 7

I wish they'd change the word love —
its used two much by the rong
pepul

Amanda aged 6

its a pity you have to
fall in love with boys because
they all ways pin ch you Beryl aged 7

I've been marrid five times, mostly with my mother, but once I did get marrid to a girl who gave me some chewing gum, But that was on holiday.

Leslie aged

My big sister fell in love And She went to this place where they Sell you holy matrimony but I Don't think she paid them all the Money because she said it wasn't woth it.

Malcolm a

My sister is always writing to Jesus an he sends her choclates an once he sent her Two lots of choclates on the same day but she won't tell me where to write.

Ian aged 6

I say my prayers with my eyes open So I can hear what I um saying.

Robin aged 5

god loves everyone who is good like me and my friend lucy but not peopul like gillian who takes other peoples rubbers

Katy aged 6